geo•logics

STEPHEN ROWE's poetry has appeared in such publications as *CV2*, *Arc Poetry Magazine*, *The Antigonish Review*, *Riddle Fence*, and many others. His first book, *Never More There* (2009), was shortlisted for the Newfoundland and Labrador Heritage and History Award. Originally from Heart's Content, he now lives in Gander.

ALSO BY STEPHEN ROWE

Never More There

geo•logics

Stephen Rowe

Breakwater Books
P.O. Box 2188, St. John's, NL, Canada, A1C 6E6
WWW.BREAKWATERBOOKS.COM

A CIP catalogue record for this book is available from Library and Archives Canada.

We acknowledge the support of the Canada Council for the Arts, which last year invested $157 million to bring the arts to Canadians throughout the country. We acknowledge the financial support of the Government of Canada through the Canada Book Fund (CBF) and the Government of Newfoundland and Labrador through the Department of Tourism, Culture and Recreation for our publishing activities.

Canada Council for the Arts Conseil des Arts du Canada

Canada

Newfoundland Labrador

PRINTED AND BOUND IN CANADA.

Breakwater Books is committed to choosing papers and materials for our books that help to protect our environment. To this end, this book is printed on a recycled paper that is certified by the Forest Stewardship Council®.

FSC www.fsc.org RECYCLED Paper made from recycled material FSC® C103567

For H, and for L

ACKNOWLEDGEMENTS

I would like to thank the editors of the following publications for their help in placing some of these poems: *Arc Poetry Magazine*, *Arts East*, *Famous Reporter*, *Paragon II*, *Rhythm Poetry Magazine*, *Riddle Fence*, *They Will Take My Island*, *Triggerfish Review*, *[Word]: A Journal of Canadian Poetry*.

I am grateful to the Newfoundland and Labrador Arts Council for funding that helped in the writing process.

"My Father's Pocket Knife," "The Doctor," and "Point of Reference" each won Newfoundland and Labrador Arts and Letters Awards in the senior poetry category.

The quotation in "Whistle" is from Al Purdy's poem "Transient."

Thank you to those who have read early versions of these poems and offered thoughts that have helped shape this book: Chris Banks, Kerri Cull, Heidi Jones, Karen Rowe, and Paul Vermeersch.

My appreciation goes to Rebecca Rose, James Langer, and everyone at Breakwater Books for their support and tireless efforts in helping make this collection a reality.

And gratitude goes to my family and friends, who inspire me to no end.

CONTENTS

A Geographic Inquiry into Loss

A Geographic Inquiry into Reason

geo•logics

A Geographic Inquiry into Loss

ONCE YOU LEAVE

you won't come back: not to those hills
mythic in sun-wash stretching to sea,
not to the sheer greens of meadows
their denizens cud-drunk with that abundance,
not to the harbour wall's gradual curve
that outreaching moon-hook of stone.

The scarp and pocked rock face will remain,
trees will hold their leaves to the same sun,
houses will creak foundations, lean away.
These things will forget you, carried
with the wind: your features strange as wanting.
They will set your form with a name

for it's been so long and the world is bent
on change, the kind that creeps a deep past
desolate of you. No you won't come back.
But someone very like you, like enough to think
those hills remain poised in welcome,
do not turn granite backs on your passing.

A MATTER OF DIMENSION

Fight

It saps your energy. The flatness, I mean. Everywhere
you tread that predictable topography, no
variation to keep the senses or your balance questioning.
On a plateau nothing changes.

Never mind the buzzing of people through streets,
the unequalled urgency of small town routines.
Soon you find the same is tied to you, worker bee,
do what you must, be where you must.

Three years the count, you never ceased to wonder
what carried you here: *experience, career*;
those easy answers come like speaking honey,
the ear and mind so far have drunk it up.

Always the grumble overhead, always the descending drone
of engines. It's expected. It's the reason
for this town, a way to harness the heavens for transport;
the dream hovers as a street light

above queues of Gander's inhabitants, while many like you,
outsiders, live in fifty-year-old houses
on pavement named for aviators; decommissioned aircraft
displayed along the main road to town;

walk through supermarkets where men and women
outfitted in military green are unknowing
reminders of a history, a present trying to shine itself
bright as narrowing rows of runway lights.

The insularity is what gets you, how you prolong
acquainting yourself: only a few roads
but you're yet to explore them all; instead stick
to required routes, say

it's for efficiency; the people you do know are colleagues
from elsewhere, guarded in conversation.
You've bunkered down, confined yourself to patterns
that have a rhythm all their own:

low-set expectation as coping mechanism, atrophy
of sense, the numbness of foot
meeting level earth. On a plateau nothing changes
until you reach the edge.

Flight

At some point you fell from home with gravity's hand
pressed on a shoulder. Standing in line
at the same café waiting for coffee you'd ordered
a hundred times before, your days

ticked off by the same faces that spiraled around you
for twenty years: a shallow indifference.
Call it boredom. Call it the same taunting body
slurred in your bed. The stagnation:

gasping in a swamp of self-regret; the temptation so easy,
unseen as it sunk in. Either way, leaving
is a matter of survival, flight a precautionary procedure,
a future for which you were wholly unprepared.

The problem with one-horse towns is a matter of
dimension: a reliance on self, pigeon-holing
scope until potential takes a single shape, prosperity
sturdy as a paper-made plane

soaring for a moment before that sudden dive.
It's all they know, it's all you know.
Your hopes narrow enough to keep you focused
as long as the short term is looking up. But

the coming down's inevitable as the daily grind,
infrastructure falls from under you
and what remains is frigid, air-lashed, an acreage
bleak as the soul you've nourished.

Extend your vision far enough and hills may begin
to rise, valleys punctuate the land story,
the slope of earth gleamed beyond horizon;
challenges of the uneven, unpredicted

become prescriptions for insanity, a cure
for cabin fever. Teeter on the edge
of a decision made; watch a mess of starlings
twist above, whipping up the world:

they feel flight in their bones, that raised habitation.
Never mind it is their nature, utterly thoughtless.
Never mind the ease with which they achieve sustained lift.
Never mind the certainty of their return.

THE CULT OF AEOLUS

Heat waves sashay above tarmac in day's
full-bodied embrace. The breeze has risen

high enough to tease out thoughts of wanton
dreaming. On this plateau the atmosphere is tangible;

the skin of a god brushed against the cheek.

Metres from the runway, cars have killed their engines:
figures face the stratosphere, anticipate the sky

falling about them, drunk on shifting pressures.
A rumble, low-*om*, from miles ahead comes

gradually, swells to a moan and a final frantic groan

metres above. Eye lids clinched they imagine letting go,
weightlessly approximating the divine, to be

dragged upward, become the mass of air. Then the
landing, wheels taxi. Each turns to leave, comes down

from this high: a taste of something wholly ambrosial.

MARTYR

it's interesting how you can brag about a scar
—Gwendolyn MacEwen

They haven't noticed what remains of the wound but you
bear it across your body, along neighbouring streets,
supermarkets, bank lines, the churchyard. Clasp it
tight before you like silverware or some grail,
swaddle it in the meaty flesh of your hands.

On trips home (they come more often now)
there's comfort in unwrapping before the family.
You know they'll listen when you tell them
what it's like to plod to work where eyes mind their own,
where architecture is dwarfed by straight-faced figures,
where the cold stones you in the street, in a place
that knows enough
to know where you're from.

Cross your arms, grip chest and neck. Like gauze
the comfort of shared segregation.
There's a story for the scar cut into you;
for the blade that made the cut, the hand that held it,
the hand that holds it still.

HABITUATION

Years in and the unspeakable happens.
Sitting in your chair the neighbourhood rises
like exhaust around you, the hardly noticed
products of time's manufacture: slow rattle of cars,
muffled screams of jet liners leaving, open
and close of the gate, sound of water as it
free falls from the eaves each time
with precision and consistency
to rap deck boards like a door, the window
blurred with light's bending. Might as well
greet mornings this way, gradual habituation sets in
like an uncle you hardly know in a stained tank top
put up in the spare room, eventually forming a fixture.
What is it you're missing? Home? No,
too easy after all this time. It's the unexpected
that haunts you, the absence of it:
how the street could easily be
your street, the town easily be your town.
You know the people strolling by, who
they are or used to be. The struggle
to belong was over before you knew it and,
shifting uncomfortably in the seat, you
reel at the thought. Home. Pan the yard
through wide French doors, survey the earth,

adjacent houses, the towering tree you
no longer notice that loomed once, a warning.
Vision settles near the patio's edge;
like last year the bleeding heart blooms,
that warm pink brighter now than ever.

THEY WILL TAKE MY ISLAND

  and gift it away with creases and folds
in coloured paper: an origami crane,
a creature of bluest possibilities stood wading
where waves once stroked the shore;

  it will satisfy their ends as only
the passive can: a coastal zoo complete with
species, quaint inhabitants, seaside villas
toured with a view of tomorrow in the offing;

  a bird aimless in the sea with a wake
broad as five hundred years of history,
each day thoughts of its hatching misting over
in the clumping North Atlantic fogs.

  And the heart's continental shelf
with its depths of longing; that legacy demands
I fold a thousand origami cranes of my own,
a siege of paper swarming crests of white, of blue.

WHAT'S LEFT BEHIND

It's what's left behind that worries you:

the narrow stretch of lane, fence-funneled,
prolonged by hesitation of crushed stone;
an assembly of lilacs, ushers in the breeze,
would gesture down the walk past the far field

to a gate profound in its purpose. Those hinges
would rasp, bemoan an awkward silence.
The tire swing clinging to memories of maple
while broad leaves drape a warm shade

(mood lighting for a distant afternoon). Wind
could breathe regret through rhubarb fingers
or hush a thousand nothings in the ear.
All it would take is a creak from that deck,

the possibility of a door left ajar.

MY FATHER'S POCKET KNIFE

My father's pocket knife rests on the dresser,
a stainless steel elongation of himself
into once knotted and grooved days I call my own.
The handle curved like the back of a German brown
he taught me to raise from rippling water
with nothing but a line and hope, the magic in his
bent form as he spoke the trout to air.
There's something exotic in the bone
that plates the handpiece in its rutted way;
perhaps walrus, perhaps caribou; a whittled relic
running with coins heard calling in his pocket.
And the blade as I extend it now (fingers
on a wishbone) can still strip the finest wire,
splice two ends so long broken
by wear and tear. That edge
as it glares the light back at me
still makes the cut, sharp and deep as ever.

DOG-WALKING AT GANDER LAKE

Labs brown and yellow wag their tails
like a sway of hands in the distance;
in search of scents, branches and refuse
lodged in crevices. Their interests
breeze-borne and transient.

Newlyweds, we foot what passes for beach,
        uneven clumps of earth,
        scattered erratics left from some
        cold dense history.

This sawblade shoreline extends
for twenty-odd miles, cuts through time
in a way that takes you off guard:

the side to side rockhopping, repetition
amplified by persistence of heat,
uneasy presence of jetsam, flotsam: the past as it
finds its way back to dry land.
Rocks themselves a mix of cultures:
        some wavepolished,
        others jagged as a heartache
linger, resilient to the flush of years.

They say no one knows how deep
she is at centre.
The mystery of it, the lake as haunting:
        lagan of silhouette, ghosts
of forgotten faces, empty spaces,
a once-bedroom, an old love forever
stagnant in the blue whose features
have degraded, become twisted with years;
the change one chooses,
        the paths unseen until tracked,
        wrecks hauled up to surface.

But the dogs have it right. They bob along,
nose a twig here, quartz crystal there,
halt to sniff a split piece of driftwood
that's idled too long on surface water

        then move further on,
        tails waving behind them.

WAKING AND REALIZING ONCE AGAIN THE CAT HAS DIED

Midnight's purple filter in the foreground,
a shifting along the walk,
                                        between slink and skulk.
The coal mass catching ripples of streetlight
like a harbour's delicate wave.
                                                Not muted,
but muting each footfall: first on concrete
then cilia of grass at the edge of the garden,
faintly detected;
                                    a sniff of the trash.
Nebulous, rolling in toward the house,
appears to stop a moment at the step,
                                                        turns
weightlessly claws the wood post and disappears
around the corner.

These breaths reach like fingers into ether,
for reassurance.
                                    I scuff laminate:
kitchen floor is cold, a draft through the back door
like something slipping in.

WAVE REFRACTION

There's the sand grit between toes
gravel-like in a foamy slush: those
minute sections of earth packed together.

We've walked this beach before,
watched tiny boaters white the waters.
A hundred yards behind, families
shake out towels,
        open car doors.

To dwell in the small spaces between,
        as we have these last years
moving from one place to another,
        bodies of sand in a wave-crush...

Over time you've come to wear me,
a collar, a tight turtleneck; feel what protects
        constrict.
The constant wrapping about headlands,
waves, their surge and surf,
        thought-shaping.

Take in the freedom here, the singular
aqueous thrust presented you like a wish:
the hooks of sea that rage,
take hold about foot and joint,
        muscle me into the undertow.
And how easy to step back, watch
separation take place, take notice
of a vastness washing away.

What of that pressure of heart
forced on your shoulders, the staggering
        shift of balance that throws you off?
A rocking sea: that steady pulse,
the relentless ache of absence.

GENTLE THE WEST WIND STIRS

Anonymous, from the Medieval Latin

Gentle the west wind stirs and the sun
climbs in its warmth. The land shows off
its curves, blurs in its own fascination.
                                        Spring begins

sheathed in purple, having adorned its own; peppers
the earth with flowers, the wild trees with leaves.
The four-footed marsh the landscape
while birds piece together nests;
they rave among blooming limbs.

The senses do their work, take in these happy wonders,
while I sigh, deep-winded.

If I raise my head while rocking alone
and do not see, do not hear these things,
an emptiness consumes me.
                              My soul tires:

Spring, consider closely
these leaves, flowers, grasses.

THE FAWN

Horace, Book I, Ode XXIII

You avoid me like a fawn that scours wild hills
for its frightened mother,
fearing the breath of gusts in a quiet forest;

for whether spring's arrival jerks the leaves,
or green lizards thrust into a bush's thorns,
it shudders in chest and knee.

Yet I do not chase you
with the tiger's savagery, a Gaetulian lion
to subdue you:

full-fledged, leave mother behind,
pursue your husband at last.

PROGRESS

Horace, Book II, Ode XV

Before long, royal buildings will leave few fields
to plough, all over ponds will be seen
as having stretched out as wide as the Lucrine Lake,
                                        the plane tree
will overcome the elms;
the beds of violets and myrtle,
                                                  sweet to the nose,
will scatter their scent to the fruitful olive-yards
of our ancestors, and the thick laurel
will block glowing sun-strikes with its boughs.

The auspices of Romulus, long-haired Cato
and our forefathers did not arrange this.
To them a private citizen held little,
                                        the public so much more;
no portico for the individual, measured out
by ten-foot poles, taking in the northern shade;
no laws permitting the fortunate to disturb
the grassy field,
                              instead directing towns
and temples of the gods to be adorned with fine
state-ordered stone.

THE HUMAN BODY IS TWO THIRDS WATER

When the flood comes fresh and thick as fear,
staining the calm of white Berber carpet—floorboards
wasted, the deep stagnancy
of rust and dirt, the sub-floor quivering,
violently moist—
                                        it's then you grasp the inner makings:
the torn tissue of foam underlay hauled up
to assess the injury, the sinew of fibreglass insulation,
the studs through which the bleeding came,
and the broken copper vessels beneath the flesh,
loosed arteries, a tightened chest.

DISRUPTION

They waked you just below the altar in a room
entirely too large for someone of your slight stature;
a short, rural church with little stained glass,
no pillars, just a few rows of pews. I saw it coming,
the death I mean, years before when you held
a reserved hand to your chest, having raised your voice
in an act of discipline for something I'd done, but
have long forgotten, while I stood above you a full
six inches or more. I was blind
to that physiological disruption of yours,
to my own small but recurrent part in it, and now
like an idiot imagine some regret in my possession
for having prevented nothing at all. As if
I could have.
                        Birthdays are a kind of purgatory,
a voice whispering strange thoughts through a year's
gaping abyss; how can we but listen to those vibrations,
drummings that fill the cavities of our auditory canals,
that echo far into the histories of ourselves?

RONDINE FOR A SLEEPLESS NIGHT

A little patience when the nighttimes smother,
encase our buzzing heads in hallowed pillows
and gales come pounding our names upon the windows.
I watch the blues of evening rush and gather,
streak along supple skin and wonder whether
you hear the whispering of pussy willows.
A little patience—

these voices outside will slow, cease, vanish. There,
as all cools, let the memories come and go
where rustles of grass once hummed between our toes.
Whatever the morning brings we'll face together.
A little patience.

NEARLY WARM

I knew you once against this cabin wall
with hair that seemed to light the alder boughs;
its winded flares tripping before my eyes.
That sun-washed smile erased the *whys* and *hows*
that etched your chin, your cheeks, made questions fall
like the splayed collar of your summer blouse,
draping woodblocks with its yellow dye.
I held your light-white skin until the call
for supper came at dusk.

But August's air
has cooled: the crooked sky now seeks its form
in the sweeping of alders tapping window glass.
Tonight the cabin's fire flickers, nearly warm,
its glow tracing the floor around this chair:
the moldered ash, those embers from the past.

THE LAUNDRY HAD TO WAIT

The laundry had to wait. Scrambling the stairs,
an excitement wracked my chest, as low or deep
as the rumble rising outside. It began a creep,
made its way down streets, a parking lot, the Sears
outlet at the mall, through drapes of rain, by chairs
on the deck out back, then settled down to sleep
like a lost dog, its roaming done. A leap
to the door to meet my wife, her dripping hair.

"The laundry had to wait." I nodded, caught
the glare of lightning in the sky and thought
tonight, perhaps, a second chance from Zeus
in recognition of our battles fought,
a downpour decreed to relieve the drought,
a humble roar to knock the door between us.

EXHUMATION

To reach a hand through snow,
to push fingers into this dirt and pull you out,

ascend the Mizzen at dawn, release your
particles from stasis
to the elemental workings of Earth,

into that great flux of life once more.

IF THEY ASK

tell them it comes like a fit of black flies
nipping in hot oppression, where you
squat through bog, knee-high in boreal mess
with the festooning of soil-slop, peat-mulch;
tell them how most mornings it feels strange
and familiar at the same time, to start a life
and abort as if forgetting were a thing of ease;
how reforming the world with sound is
a kind of tectonic force, profound thought-plates
drift into position, an order preordained
by no one in particular;
                                        tell them
there's nothing like failing a thousand times
then flailing your thoughts through the gutter,
slaying the versions of self created
with each mouthing of word and oath; how
to get the job done you release the locust,
plagues of cicadas that swarm ethereal forest,
then wait for each to find its one true place
among millions that live, die, and feed the earth.

A Geographic Inquiry into Reason

MEDITATION IN WINTER

There is virtue in thought, the rational kind
that comes deliberate as a Sunday morning:
force of light through a glass pane,
persistence in the wind's marathon,
the certainty of January's loitered chill;
the working-out of action.

If the mercury's low, then a coat for sure.
From an open door the vapour of my breath
drifts on sloshes of air. Zipped-up,
I take the snowflake on my shoulder,
find the stoic nature of its
downward embrace as sensible as blood
caressing vein-walls,

as sensible as indifferent truth:

the roses have been exiled (the season's edict);
the poplar once fully clothed in twittering green

is no less than it was all those months ago.

I assess the season's blanched sprawl:
this yard's a thing of beauty, strung
by nature's compelling minutia

and what remains for me to do.

THE SNOW

does not care. Its molecules of water
crystallized at some distant altitude, shaped
by absence of heat, abundance of vapour,
a divine atmospheric hand; those intricate
structures fashioned from the externals
that whisk about in the flake's forging.

The snow does not care that at a point,
unclear to itself, it will descend,
whitewash the sky, meander
to earth, tossed from drift
to drift then settle. Snow cares only that it
is as it can be: puritan of white.

COMPACTION

When you get angry, you should know that you aren't guilty of an isolated lapse, you've encouraged a trend and thrown fuel on the fire.
—Epictetus, *Discourses,* Book II

It begins somewhere in the brain's storage,
    a thought initially that diminishes by the week,
something of only the slightest consideration.
    Attention on hiatus: you've forgotten the dishes,
let floors hoard the random sheddings of dogs,
    sat by while snow, once newly drifted
into whitecaps along the walkway's drowning,
    undergoes the season's gradual compaction.
Already you've begun to feel the drawing-down
    of shoulder, the long drag of the heel
and, when evening lays its bloodless hands
    upon you, realize you're not ready for it;
that trial of priorities leading inevitably
    to the car and a cloudless night alone,
a bed half filled by your counterpart in strife.
    Let it go. But this response has been learned;
validating the self against all exteriors: a passion
    with a kindling potential to burn the mind.

And where has it gotten you? Jailed in fleece
    behind the wheel of a car yet in park,
a wide and true darkness shackling the dash,
    above which the distant stars bear down.

THE GREAT MACEDONIAN

an annotation for Seneca's On Benefits

Alexander, with phalanxes of spear-shielded hoplites,
marching canopies of bronze and iron, marrow crushing cavalry,
scattered deifications of himself across the sand-swept world,
constructed self-titled cities to light the candles of his honour,
appointed governors in his wake to fill the satrapies
of empire. Dipped his hand in the spirit of the River Indus
and it was done. But one man declined the gift of city,
bowed before the conqueror and offered up his reasons.
Alexander replied, *I do not ask what is becoming for you to receive,*
but what is becoming for me to give. He turned then to stand
before spear-won Persia's townships, construed as pews,
his benefits handed out, freedoms gifted from one to another.

THE DEATH OF SENECA

after Peter Paul Rubens

To preserve himself he cuts his wrists, lets blood
from old arteries dye his toga, all the while
looking skyward, philosophy a constellation.
Gathered about him: servants to work the act through,
a scribe to take dictation of his terribly important
words, Nero's praetorians over his shoulder
to enforce a drawn out death, grimacing.
Physician and friend Statius Annaeus holds him,
considers poison to speed expiry. The man's
defined tendons and muscle,
the care taken of body into age.

Seneca above the water basin,
                                        his failing knees, reaching a hand
into anguish, toward the next chamber,
                                                                an open doorway:
his wife flowing into red wrists of her own.

MIST

From the porch, movement is subtle
but everywhere. In the drizzle, green leaves
twitter from the silver poplar, stalks of grass jerk
yet more growth as their season prepares
for the metamorphosis. The dog takes a piss
under a rose bush that once blossomed pink
but still provides relief from the once deluge.
On the shed door an orb spinner's web hangs heavy
with beads of dew, interwoven crystal necklaces
that sway ever so gently in the morning grey.
There's reason behind it all, some force
of will nearly escaping the senses. Seek it out.
Look to petals of rain, the nature
shared between them. Their lot to fall, to drop,
the atmosphere releasing them as from a womb.
There's no fighting it so they plummet, make
the most of that brief time, in their billions
collide with leaf, grass blade, deck, an upturned palm.
As you peer into the distance through all those
microprisms, mirrors gleaming at the world,
the mist lingers thick as thought.

BIRTH SONG FOR EPICTETUS

Your mother was a slave. This her immortality:
an ancient inscription drifting through time's ether,
a singular fact lingering like a familiar scent.

We know nothing of the conception: fingernails
furrowing your father's sweat-glistened skin, his
inelegant thrusting, how it must have been

longer or shorter than expected; the smell of oil alight
in a lamp nearby, the absence thereof, the features
of his face and name. We can't begin the tricky

guesswork of love. A hand taken willingly in hand,
or a master's final evocation of title; another load
to weigh on her as she brought his morning meal.

There's no telling the difficulty of gestation, if
shame or worry held any significance. Reality is
she birthed you. In some deep recess of Hieropolis

you broke to day's abundance or night's lack
or something in between, nearly breaking her:
the fissure of her quaking thighs, the laboured

eruption of blood and fluid and child into arms
quivering for you. Was there a man to stand
by her? An outward manifestation of the strength

she held? Or perhaps she preferred to go alone
through the valley of your days, that final elision:
an etching of man or god to crease her face.

SURE-ROOTED

As morning lays a calloused hand upon you
through the blinds, vertigo takes you
from dreaming the night amniotic to the blink
reflex that comes of a sudden waking light.
Outside, spring gestates: a white-bellied garden
and green burst nearly carried to term and you
coming to terms with it. There's derision
in its predictability; nature's inability to miscarry,
the way she flaunts herself as poster-girl
for the perfect womb. How, mindlessly, she rubs it in.
Biological imperative lost on you, the world a party
to which you're not invited. Trees, grasses,
spring birds in the distance, two labs on the bed;
even rock reforms itself in eruptions of molten thought.
Everywhere vision settles there's the same question
and something missing, something placental
that would fasten you to the rest of existence,
corded to the waist to keep you steady, grounded
like the peony deep in the garden, snow-sheathed,
swelling, sure-rooted in wait for bloom time.

IN THE DAWN THERE IS A LEANING

of breeze on grass shoulder, whispers of alder
branch and birch, gooweddy's pink corsage;

of imperfect geometries on hand-raised wharf,
bowline taught, the red cabin at Cowards Island;

of sunglare on hill-stretch, swooping field.
A promontory into blanched sky:

you with PJs and ponytail,
sitting cross-legged
on the edge of my waking.

POEM AT CAPE SPEAR

There is no mild yoke for the living.
I haul myself as in pails of hard water,
slosh the many dissolved minerals of my bones;
each gradual spill an unburdening.
But it's never enough as I try my damnedest
through moss and root, over bog and rock,
with the lighthouse beacon still far atop the hill,
to find some place to lay down these shoulders
where the daily sloughing goes unnoticed.
Some thirty years of sea-blown sand and dirt
have known me, like a stone-bottomed sack
this island; in the depths of the boreal forest
stand parts of me cast off in moulting,
silhouetted figures that linger beyond the fog.

At last this new ground: the spruce and fir behind,
the eroding soil that holds for the moment,
and, a hundred feet below, the red jags are smashed
with the nagging question of waves.

WEEDING

Somewhere in the backlog you'll find the sprouting,
sparse at first, spread like an infection unchecked.
Before you knew it they'd taken over, entangled
thoughts, leaving you with fixed patterns of cognition.
From a window you peer into the garden
where they rise through tattered earth. Tell yourself
they can't really choke the tulips, but you swear
those stems lean in too close. Their stranglehold
on logic tight as your grip on the weeder. Press those prongs
into the ground, grasp the root and pull. Reasoned
efficiency is key, cleanses the mind; ambling thoughts
plucked and discarded somewhere deep in the landfill.
Once your guard is up it must not fall by the wayside:
extraction brings order, one dead dandelion at a time.

CONSOLATIONS

1. If human experience has a beginning, it must have an end;
you and I once were;
so you and I are not.

2. If human experience has a beginning, it must have an end;
you and I are not;
so you and I may be.

3. Either this evening passes slowly, or your memory remains;
time preserves its pace regardless of you or I;
so the darkness settles over me with a shiver.

4. Our freedoms cannot be shared, our past fetters as they are;
below you: a world diminishing in the sun;
below me: manacles of stone, fossil-forged.

5. If you glanced down upon the rocks, I would take it as a sign;
after all this time I still divine among granite and basalt;
the gleam of your eyes alien to me.

6. Can I control the dancing of your hair, or the memory?
I think of light strands that slip through my fingers;
somewhere the elements pattern you differently.

7. Not you and I;
not you;
so I.

8. I cannot be both composer and player of my life's score.
Song is taken through the strings with my fingers' prayer;
we're more a part of fate than faith can allow.

9. If pond water stagnates, less erosion occurs;
you wade through murky me-less days, boots firm in silt;
expression unworn.

10. Either you change or I;
I run down the lane, arms overflowing with our pieces;
You remain at the corner, thumb out.

POINT OF REFERENCE

Western Brook Beach, NL

Never mind the river that walks you down to shore
ever dedicated to its faithful pilgrimage of water,
the hard-won shape worn into rock and pebble;
never mind how all of a sudden the earth weathers to
grains beneath your feet, demanding sandals come off;
the ripping sound of waves (louder you swear than
anything you've heard) wash in on the wind as you
trek dunes on a spit slung out into sea;
never mind the tiny shells between your toes
or the sun-fire that bears down, a bishop's hand
on the head, confirming in that moment all things;
and never mind, as you lay for hours in the sand,
those miniscule pieces of earth brushing your face,
that have made the same immeasurable journey
from whatever life they knew to this very point
where the four elements twist and blend around you;
rather mind the larger pieces of stone that line the river,
scramble to collect their round, denuded edges,
place them one atop another, an inuksuk marking
this place, your time here, the long way back.

WHISTLE

Molly forces air through the whistle
of her snout and, though she sounds
stuck in a loop, tired and repetitive
as the proverbial record, she whines with desire,
an urgency lost on me.
She's placed in mind a factory,
one I've only seen in a documentary:
some manufacturing to be done, thoughts
on a conveyor moving down the line.
A great collective sigh is heard
over the winding-down machines
as she blows the signal that ends a day.
Or even the long steam draw
of a train headed nowhere in particular.
But it could never be just some train
directed by steel guidelines, rather
a train stressing the point that I've
never been on a train. But there: myself a passenger,
a transient in the ambling red glow of a sun
that never moves, leaving slashes of itself
on bare tree, boulder, a pretty girl's heavy face.
That screech again and it's another's train,
his voice rumbling down the line:
you are where you were always going.

And what fascinates me to no end:
that a yellow lab with a nervous disposition
can get it right, can know the want inherent
in a simple sound made on impulse
at the very second it's required;
how I, reading poems behind a closed door,
have deprived her of the one thing she needs;
how she, whining as she does,
deprives me of so much more.

AN EYE'S BLINK

For we are made for co-operation, like feet, like hands,
like eyelids, like the rows of upper and lower teeth.
—Marcus Aurelius, *Meditations*, Book II

For so long I'd thought those feet tangled,
awkward double left-footedness. Interaction
akin to running a three-legged race, the struggle
inherent in unerring simultaneous motion,

in seeing eye-to-eye: the difficulty in the grace
of an eye's blink; to make this our daily work,
to hold always the form of another's face
in the wink of a butterfly's fabric wing; not to shirk

our sewn natures. I, the needle to your cloth: fine
for me to say, to push that gentle pulse of breath
through lips, past rows of upper and lower teeth, lines
that work together, grind against each other.

THE DOCTOR

Father used to talk about him.
An odd man in round-rim glasses
bold and black, held perpetually
high on the nose. A dapple grey
cantering through the long grass
of his hair, not quite shoulder length,
tripping eccentric.

Saturday nights at the Legion
playing crib with bachelors.
Scotch on the bar, smoke to his lips,
looking for a 4-5-6 run,
lecturing on Yeats, the wonder of war,
what baby he'd birthed that morning
and the value of a good dog,
his own a mastiff large and sluggish
that never left his side.
The game over, he'd leave on a high note,
the animal his shadow.

When the time came he,
in withered old age,

pronounced my grandmother's death
much as he did her name;
the hint of a summer breeze

Winnie
Winnie

The repetition just to be sure,
his pulse a racing of hooves.

That night he had a drink or two with the old man
who never spoke of his death weeks later,
preferred their card games instead.
Never the half glass of scotch
resting on the end table, the rocking chair,

his long hair parted to the side, a hole
in his face where the bullet went.
The old mastiff staring doorward,
inconsolably prostrate across veined feet,
refused to move an inch
even when the constable came.

AUTUMN

The steady descent of nature: temperature
presses down the mercury, water pellets
soil where it once was raised in heat,
the apple tree out back loses its namesake,
fruit of the season, this *Fall.*

The leaves know it, this gradual coming
down from some high, some point of heaven
(or nearly so). For a time attached to a gnarled
branch, life giver. Intravenous flow then
break away, make an end.

And then to know what's in store: make
one twist after another in the hands of sky,
or a child's climbing, to take that inevitable
freefall tumble, then the nutrient breakdown
of you, spirited creature of earth:

is it a giving back, reciprocity, a grand *thank you*
for the chance to live something, anything
for an undetermined period? Or perhaps
a tiny role, a quivering piece of nature lent you
that wasn't yours to start with.

CUP

Begin with the teacup, how it lies
half full on the desk, resting its floral patterned
laurels on the rutted chestnut surface,
the stain rings collected like brown leaves of autumn
come once from some distant upholding;
take it between the creases of your fingers and marvel
at the sudden transformation,
the past that rises through flared nostrils: Nan's kitchen
and the wood smoke musk brushing aside
October's chill, the plastic potted daisies in the corner,
the wallpaper itself striped in a design
from the garden, violets and wild tiger lilies,
knuckles crippled around the handle
of a half-empty vessel not unlike your own, steaming;
then drink before it becomes too much,
taste the tea leaf essence that lingers on the tongue,
has soaked into the part of you that stands
where a dark wood floor creaked twenty years ago,
where everything was as you make it now.

THE HARVESTERS

after Pieter Brueghel

They scythe the gold leaf wheat,
the straight-cut walls of their effort
that glimmer before the sickle blade in a sky
easy on sun. The felling of their work
weighs on the curves of their shoulders,
the harvest plotted behind. Each arc-swung reaping
gives way to another, a cropped incline
wrought to the town's edge. Beyond that
another slope rising yellow into haze.
Women and men bent low behind the hewers
tie sheaves from the newly shaved field,
flick sweat like fertilizer across spent soil.
The bundles up-righted like homes,
like stones to mark a dying-place.

TOUCH

There is no forgiveness in the falling
of leaves. At once complete and partial,
ready and not ready. In the clasp of currents
they break with the world in ending, severed
at the petiole; that tactile sense a memory.

As they burn about you, show a little pity,
look into the great vagary of sky, see
their last moments as themselves. To these martyrs
hold out the stems of your hands, the yet living
parts of earth; for them reach, reach.